One Minute
with GOD

HOPE LYDA

HARVEST HOUSE PUBLISHERS

EUGENE, OREGON

ONE MINUT
Copyright © 2
Published by H
Eugene, Orego
www.harvesthc

ISBN-13: 978-0-7369-2166-4
ISBN-10: 0-7369-2166-4

Printed in the United States of America
08 09 10 11 12 13 14 15 16 / BP-NI / 10 9 8 7 6 5 4 3 2 1

Contents

In a Minute

In 60 seconds you can…floss your teeth, feed a parking meter, tie your shoes, ignore the call of a telemarketer, order take-out Chinese, oh yeah, and fulfill your life purpose.

Really.

If you've ever questioned what the point of life is, I can tell you the answer right here and now: it is to spend time with God and to know him personally through moments of elation and times of difficulty, bits of minutia and stretches of meaningful living.

Every 60 seconds is an opportunity to think on what matters, deepen faith, converse with God, embrace the big and small celebrations, love others, and be awake for your own life. I consider these "miracle minutes," because before you know it, they transform into longer, fluent sessions of prayer, gratitude, and awareness—they become a lifetime spent with God.

Belief

Words for Belief

I trust in your unfailing love;
my heart rejoices in your salvation.

PSALM 13:5

Trust in the LORD and do good;
dwell in the land and enjoy safe pasture.
Delight yourself in the LORD
and he will give you the
desires of your heart.

PSALM 37:3-4

Commit your way to the LORD;
trust in him and he will do this:
He will make your righteousness
shine like the dawn,
the justice of your cause
like the noonday sun.

PSALM 37:5-6

Blessed is the man who makes
the LORD his trust,
who does not look to the proud,
to those who turn aside to false gods.

When I am afraid, I will trust in you.
In God, whose word I praise,
in God I trust; I will not be afraid.
What can mortal man do to me?

PSALM 56:3-4

Look, you are trusting in deceptive
words that are worthless.

JEREMIAH 7:8

In him and through faith in
him we may approach God with
freedom and confidence.

EPHESIANS 3:12

Reaching for Faith

When I stand my ground and insist that belief has not worked, that faith has let me down, it is usually after I have taken a tumble. Wouldn't faith in God—wouldn't God for that matter—make sure that I didn't end up here again…in the mess of mistake and regret.

But even the huge blind spot of my denial is not big enough, or permanent enough, for me to eventually see that it was my doing that led to my undoing. Sometimes I can even see the life rafts, wake-up calls, or yield signs God provided. Don't let belief become your scapegoat. If you believe, walk in it. And when you fall, cling to it.

———

I'm sitting here in the middle of my latest mistake. I want to blame you for my frailty when actually it is my fragile state of life that gives me the greatest insight into your presence. Lead me toward belief in my purpose so that I can let go of excuses and reach for faith.

Faith Thesaurus

My family watches a popular game show because it is all about words. It is fun to fill in some of the missing letters and guess the word or phrase that is up on the screen with a few gaping holes in it. It also challenges one's mind to think through more words and to learn new ones along the way.

Are you spending time searching for words that fill you and feed you? The other words—ones that belittle, reject, and negate life and God's children—are all around you. So all the more reason to expand your personal thesaurus of positivisms; you can share goodness, peace, hope, encouragement, acceptance, and belief every time it's your turn!

Clean up my language, Lord. I use so many negative expressions and share so much of my inner turmoil, that I bypass all the joy and the good things I know. I want to pass along the words of strength, power, love, and forgiveness you give to me. You are the Word—may I express you every day.

Radiant Faith

We replaced our heater with a blower because it was loud, used up a lot of energy, and was either on or off, rather than constantly emanating warmth. Now we have a radiant heater placed in the corner of our living room that warms our old house during winter.

The way we share our faith can be a lot like these forms of heat. Some people are "on" all the time and loud about their faith. This kind of witness can be powerful, but it can also feel forced rather than authentic. When you are strong in your belief, you can stand quietly among others and still radiate the warmth of faith—peace, love, kindness, truth.

❖

Help me radiate with your love. When I force my
beliefs and become loud about my righteousness,
it is usually all about me, and not about you.
I want my life to emit the serenity, mercy, and
warmth I receive unconditionally from you.

Even in the Unknowing

When television shows, news segments, or Internet highlights present the hard and sad things going on near or far, our feelings of distress can be so overwhelming that we forget to rest in God. We can turn our anxiety over to God in prayer. He's already on it, you can be sure. And the more we give our fears up to God's care, the better able we are to embrace peace and hope and act on our compassion and empathy.

How we face the unknowns can build up or dismantle the foundation of faith. We can't be sure what tomorrow will bring to us and to others in the world, but we can find our solid footing in the known, in the absolutes of God's faithfulness.

❖

God, I want to feel for those in pain. I want to rise up and speak for those who face injustice. I want to be strong for those who are fragile. To do these things, I must first trust you. May I stop trembling in my insecurities here on the bridge of fear and cross to the safe refuge of your understanding. You don't ask me to know all or be prepared for every possible happening; you ask only that I believe, and that I move forward in that belief.

Staying Focused

Who, what, where, when, how? Our minds sift through these questions constantly. We are always on a quest for answers. Big or small, these questions often end up directing our lives. But shouldn't the answers be what guide our steps? How long do you wait for word from God before you start asking more questions or create an answer of your own?

As we continue to ask questions, we will learn and grow. But we will be blessed when we pause long enough to listen for what God is saying.

❖

I so want to know the future and my purpose and the outcome to decisions I made a week ago, last year...God, help me stay focused on the priorities you give me right now. Grant me the patience and the courage to move forward even when question marks fill my thoughts. It is enough that I know the One who holds all the answers.

Heartbreak Belief

Has love ever come at a price in your life? What has been your experience? Love certainly requires sacrifice; that is to be expected. What we don't anticipate are the times when love breaks us or breaks our trust. It is difficult to consider loving again until healing comes.

God heals us with saving grace. Divine faithfulness mends torn trusts; our identity becomes tied to wholeness rather than wrapped up in broken dreams. Your spiritual heart is not lost, nor is it dangling by a man-made, fragile thread. It is intact and connected to God's heart. Love does come at a price, but the price has been paid.

❖

You've been with me through my heartache. There were times I could barely breathe. I know that you carried me. Even now, you are still carrying me through and over the remains of past pain. Thank you for never losing sight of me. I felt so small, insignificant, and lost. You held me in your hand so that I would feel the strength and power of true love.

How Do I Look?

If we do an abdominal workout every day for one month, we kinda hope someone notices. If we have our hair cut in a new style, we want to look fresh. Yet when we spend time in devotions, prayer, and fellowship, are we expecting results? Are we anticipating that a noticeable change will occur? We should.

When we nurture our spiritual lives, there will be an outward manifestation of a renewed, stronger faith. "The fruit of the Spirit is love, joy, peace, patience, kindness, goodness, faithfulness, gentleness and self-control" (Galatians 5:22-23). The results of spiritual growth go beyond our hearts and souls and become visible as the harvest is lived out.

God, help me remember that a renewed
mind and heart should be visible as I practice
patience and self-control, express kindness,
turn toward love and joy, speak for peace, act
out of faithfulness, and offer gentleness.

Miracle of Belief

To expand my faith, I decided to pay attention to all the miracles around me and to determine which was the greatest. I noted the countless little blooms on each lilac, the shadows cast by the sun, the intricacy of the human eye, a friend's comment that brought me awareness and comfort. The list was endless as soon as it began.

With God's fingerprints everywhere I looked, it occurred to me what the greatest miracle was—out of thin air, completely real, and the one thing that tied me to all the miracles—my belief.

Thank you for my belief. Through years of questions and private doubts, I feel the depth of the miracle of faith. It gives me new life, new eyes for your work, and a heart that knows its Maker.

Perseverance

Words for Perseverance

Love the LORD your God with all
your heart and with all your soul
and with all your strength.

DEUTERONOMY 6:5

The fear of the LORD is the
beginning of wisdom;
all who follow his precepts have
good understanding.
To him belongs eternal praise.

PSALM 111:10

Great is our Lord and mighty in power;
his understanding has no limit.
The LORD sustains the humble
but casts the wicked to the ground.

PSALM 147:5-6

The LORD is my strength and my shield;
my heart trusts in him, and I am helped.

PSALM 28:7

The LORD gives strength to his people;
the LORD blesses his people with peace.

PSALM 29:11

When Pilate heard this, he was even
more afraid, and he went back inside the
palace. "Where do you come from?" he
asked Jesus, but Jesus gave him no answer.
"Do you refuse to speak to me?" Pilate
said. "Don't you realize I have power
either to free you or to crucify you?"

JOHN 19:8-10

What Now?

Have you reached your "what now" point? It's pretty easy to recognize; in fact, you may have been here before. It happens when your cleverness and education and Internet-search savvy stop being enough to get by. You've tapped all your resources to solve a problem, create a different outcome, or make a change.

"What now" can be a very fruitful time of awakening. Use it to embrace your limits rather than resist them, and turn to God's strength for whatever is next.

Okay, God, I am here. I've tried everything, and I know I can't fix my life or even my current situation. I should've learned this lesson years ago, but I resisted it. I want to trust in your strength. I want to face whatever is next and know that you're in control.

All We Need

The more you know about God, the more you know you need God. A desire to be faithful, righteous, and godly leads us to the Cross. When difficulties rise up, our hearts know where home is. We long for communion with God and the comfort of his leading. We seek his wisdom and truths so that our lives are based on solid ground.

We tend to look at a need as something that is missing, when really our needs are our stepping stones back to God's love and guidance. Our lack is his abundance. Our doubt is his assurance. And our weakness is his strength.

Take me to your heart, God. I want to just be in your presence so that I can know you better. My wants tend to lead me back to myself. My needs direct me back to you, my Creator. Only you truly know what I need to carry on.

Leapin' Faith

Kids like to take flying leaps from edges of pools, jungle gyms, or stairs and holler "Catch me." Sometimes their request is said too late, or their weight and enthusiasm creates an uncatchable human cannonball. Not good.

There is a fruitful time and place for us to throw ourselves on God's strength. I suppose anytime is still considered a leap of faith, but when we do it in the midst of dire straits or midjump after *we've* made a big decision without his earlier input, we are really testing the limits of reality more than we are giving ourselves over to God's strength and purpose. Are you at a place of decision? Try praying "Catch me" *before* you are midflight.

———◆———

I'm so close to leaping. I think on things for so very long that I begin to lose my nerve. Now I can barely hold myself back. God, please give me the patience to wait on your guidance and direction. Give me peace and leading before I jump into a decision made by me on my terms.

The Great Exchange

It only takes me a couple of visits to the gym to realize how limited my physical strength is. And it only takes me a couple of exposures to trials to realize how limited my spiritual and emotional strength is. Thank goodness that we are supposed to hand over our measly human power and exchange it for God's might.

We might want to use God like an on-call personal trainer or life coach, but when we do, we are still holding on to our limited version of life. Give over what you've got, and take on the amazing, boundless power of God.

⬩⬩⬩

*I'm handing over my very limited strength, God.
I've given things my best effort and have realized
that you want something even more for me than
the results I've managed. I only see what is humanly
possible; you see what is ultimately possible.*

Reaching Higher

I know it is easy to think you can do it all on your own. Sometimes that is exactly how we get as far as we do—because we are independent and have had to stand alone for whatever reason. This personal gusto and ambition can light a fire under the human spirit, but the good news about your life of faith is that it is ignited by the Holy Spirit.

Faith isn't asking for a handout or even a hand up; it is acknowledging that you are not standing alone, but on the shoulders of God.

❖

Faith has helped me get to where I am. But my lack of faith has kept me from reaching beyond my abilities. I'm desperately in need of your shoulders to stand on. It is tough to lose my footing on the earth, but I want my reach to be that much closer to the sky.

Let Your Heart Lead

When I get really stressed, my thoughts become scattered. I'm forgetful. My words get jumbled, I can't listen to what others are saying, and my logic is less than solid. When I do speak a full sentence, I can be insensitive without knowing it. Have you been there?

When your mind is preoccupied or taken over by stress-brain, it is more important than ever to spend time in prayer. Becoming centered on God and his presence will still the emotions, the spinning thoughts, and the panic. So don't worry. The next time your mind is juggling life's details badly, go to your heart for answers.

God, I'm spending time here in my heart with you. I like the peace, the inspiration, and the comfort that fills me. So often I come to you with just my thoughts, my data from the day; may I learn to start from my heart so that I am capable of hearing you clearly.

Beyond Our Limits

After many years of dependence on glasses, I couldn't wait to have lasik eye surgery. Immediately after, I could see the clock on the wall. Within days I drove to the coast. But months later when I couldn't see the writing on a sign aisles away at a store, I was disappointed—my miracle had blurry edges—until a friend with glasses said she couldn't even see the sign.

As with our vision, our human perspective will always have limits. God's clarity is forever. There are no cloudy moments. God knows truth beyond our deepest questions. God sees beyond our blurry, short-sighted goals. God's understanding has no limit.

———◆———

You see all, know all, and understand all. My vision is so limited. As I push on toward my immediate goals and my next destination, I cannot see up ahead. I must trust you and entrust to you my entire journey.

Let Go My Ego

Have you ever faced a challenge head-on and left God out of it? Do you sometimes let doubt lead you back to self-reliance? It is human to have questions and even to question God. But when you offer up your strength and ability as the solution rather than trust God, you will keep running into yourself and the same ol' problems you always bring to the table.

The strength of the Almighty is working through you. Don't miss out on it!

❦

Lord, stop me from interfering so much. I want to take over every situation. Figuring out faith is hard. Forgive me when I take a shortcut by trying to do it my way. I promise to come to you with my doubts and concerns. When my ego tries to take your place, remind me how that tends to get me in trouble!

In the Will

What would you do or say or overcome in order to be first in line for a large family inheritance? This might be a theme for numerous Hollywood films, but it isn't presented to many of us in real life. Too bad. Or is it?

Real security isn't about getting in the good graces of a wealthy distant relative. Thank goodness we have a wealthy, close God. His abundance is given freely to all his children. Struggles will come, but they will be used toward growing a deeper faith and a greater understanding of grace. When we place our hope in God's strength, our future security is immediate.

I love that as I seek and walk in your will, I am in your eternal will—I have an inheritance that surpasses earthly dollars. There is so much more security and peace of mind and spirit that comes with the legacy of your grace and compassion.

Waiting Rooms

I've had my share of hospital waiting rooms lately. I'm not a fan. Thankfully some hospitals now have pagers, similar to those handed out at restaurants on a Saturday night, with flashing lights to announce your spot in the medical lineup. I like them because they are a pass to step beyond the sliding doors and into the sun where I can breathe.

Our faith is a pass to more hopeful times of waiting. We still go through the experience, but it is less about enduring and more about nurturing and understanding. Let God show you a new way to persevere. The light we hold from him gives freedom and rest.

———◆———

You know I hate to wait. I was about to implode when a new perspective of faith came to me. I finally understood that when I'm waiting, I'm not restricted to a sterile, unnourished life. You still cover me, you carry me, and you calm my impatient spirit.

Joy

Words for Joy

The LORD your God will bless you in all
your harvest and in all the work of your
hands, and your joy will be complete.

DEUTERONOMY 16:15

Nehemiah said, "Go and enjoy choice
food and sweet drinks, and send some to
those who have nothing prepared. This
day is sacred to our Lord. Do not grieve,
for the joy of the LORD is your strength."

NEHEMIAH 8:10

You make me glad by your deeds, O LORD;
I sing for joy at the works of your hands.

PSALM 92:4

Those who sow in tears
will reap with songs of joy.

PSALM 126:5

A man finds joy in giving an apt reply—
and how good is a timely word!

PROVERBS 15:23

————◆————

I have told you this so that my joy may be in
you and that your joy may be complete.

JOHN 15:11

————◆————

Out of the most severe trial, their
overflowing joy and their extreme
poverty welled up in rich generosity.

2 CORINTHIANS 8:2

————◆————

In all my prayers for all of you,
I always pray with joy.

PHILIPPIANS 1:4

————◆————

Good Times

It is healing to laugh. A good movie, a great conversation, or a comic moment can lift my spirits. I feel physically lighter and more hopeful when laughter has been a part of my day. I can be facing big challenges, and yet the mere recollection of a funny incident can shift everything toward hope.

Joy can give us that ongoing path toward hope. It isn't dependent upon humor but is inspired by faith and contentment. It is a brightness that does not fade.

———◆———

Thank you for the gift of laughter. When it comes along, I am reminded of the simplicity of pure happiness. Show me how I can go beyond occasional moments of lightness to an ongoing, ever-flowing sense of joy and peace.

Generate Joy

Do you light up a room when you walk in? Okay, do you make others feel accepted and appreciated? Does your attitude express your faith, or does it keep others at a distance? As people of faith, we don't always have to be "on," and we don't have to present a perfect life. But we will live a more meaningful life if we generate joy around us through genuine kindness and interest in the well-being of others.

Your light can be a simple greeting, an offer of help, a warm welcome.

God, nudge me when I have a chance to extend friendship to another. Open my eyes to the times when others are reaching out to me. I want to see each person just as you do. Help me sense their heart needs so that I can respond with kindness and thoughtfulness.

What You Make It

I have a lot of deadlines. I need to get to the dentist. The vet keeps sending me postcards for my cats' annual shots. My car needs an oil change. And I haven't gone grocery shopping in two weeks. Some days when I'm scrambling to stay afloat, I have to ask "Shouldn't there be more to my life experience?"

There it is. Like a life raft floating within reach—joy. Buoyant. Available. Just waiting for me to grab hold of it. As responsibilities rise and fall like waves around me, I am able to stay afloat. I feel lighter. And the view from this particular day, this moment, is sacred.

Forgive me for focusing so much on the work of living that I forget to celebrate the wonder and joy. You have made the life experience complex and overflowing with goodness. Help me grab hold of the mystery and the delight of being alive.

Grief Encounter

Sorrow can seep into the body, the mind, and the spirit. It can settle in between our bones and thoughts and drift into our dreams. When our journey takes us through grief, our cries rise up beyond our physical life and become prayers for peace. God hears us and leads our hearts toward the possibility of transformation.

As we turn over our sorrow to God's care, our weeping turns to song. Our mourning turns to joy. Our brokenness turns to wholeness. Our poverty of spirit turns to wealth of hope.

———◆———

God, I can't see beyond the hurt right now. I'm entrusting the pain and the loss to your hands. It is a relief to know that even when I don't know what to say, you hear my cries, and you prepare a way for me to find peace once again.

Praise

God amazes me. He baffles me too, but mostly he surprises me with the incredible moments of happiness that come my way. I want to praise God when the wave of joy floods my being. Like a parent beaming at the sight of her baby's smile, God must also connect to his children's pleasure with equal joy.

When delight brightens your countenance, turn your face upward in gratitude—your heart will follow, and you will see a reflection of God's gladness.

With all the joys I savor in life, may I remember to lift up my gladness to you in praise. Those moments of deep delight are a gift. Help me to acknowledge them and to hold them close so that the echoes of each joy stay with me through the days of my life.

After Party

Trials will befall our paths and the paths of those we love most. What I'm discovering is that after the trials there does come a time of relief and joy. When you aren't expecting it, flashes of happiness surface after a long absence.

You might not even know how to respond to joy because it is in such contrast to the hardship. But God does lead you out of the desert of loss or trouble. He invites your spirit to reawaken to joy so that you can celebrate the blessing of his love through the journey and on the other side of this hardship.

———

I'm not ready for balloons and party invitations. I ache inside, and I have days that seem covered in clouds. But I'm beginning to feel again—the hurt is there, but it has made room for moments of peace, and they are so refreshing. Thank you for remembering me, God. Thank you for restoring my capacity for joy.

Thinking of You

Who brings a smile to your face? Who was the one who gave you confidence to reach for your dreams? Who offered you help and empathy when you felt so alone? Consider the many friends and strangers God has brought to your experience. It does the spirit good to think about the times you felt deep connection to God through another human being.

Take time to reflect fondly on those people who have touched your life. It does the heart wonders to realize that your joy is their joy, their happiness is your happiness. This is community, this is fellowship, this is God.

How have I forgotten the lovely people you have brought me closer to in one way or another? It is such a gift to think of past friends or mentors or even role models I've never met. God, today I lift up those people and pray joy for their lives.

Let Loose

Something changes in my spirit when a laugh or a smile emerges seemingly out of nowhere. Suddenly all the adult pressures are gone. I used to squelch the strong impulses of joy, because they can come over me when I should be focused, or serious, or worried, or in charge. I'm learning to loosen up and embrace each time joy shines on my life.

As a child, did you laugh a lot with a certain friend, or find great happiness when a teacher helped you tap in to a passion for learning, or stare with fascination at a ladybug resting on your flip-flop in the summer sun? Don't restrict your happiness…recapture the pure joy of living!

———

Why don't I let myself enjoy life more? Since when does growing up mean giving up abundant, pleasurable living? No more! I promise to indulge in laughter and contentment, God. The delights of being your child are too great to count, so I will gather what I can and say thank you!

Rearview-Mirror Lessons

When I think back over my life, there were times when worries about my work, an important decision, or the future occupied my every thought. Each concern seemed like it was the biggest and most pivotal fork in the road I would ever face. Now I understand that God does carry us through these worries.

What seems insurmountable today may very well be tomorrow's testimony of joy. Hindsight is a great teacher. Each stumbling block becomes another opportunity to trust God. Let today's burden transform to blessing as you give it over to God's care.

———◆———

I've gotta say, I'm ready for this current burden to become a lesson learned, a story of faith, a past trial I lean upon for new strength. But as much as I want it to be over, God, I know that you are calling me to be very present, aware, awake, and faithful while this hardship unfolds.

Joy Full

What fills you? What interests, gifts, talents, passions, and dreams inspire you? There are so many activities and details that deplete our energy and happiness reserves, making it vital to understand what things or people or pursuits fill us back up.

God's love is an endless source of hope and contentment. Once you begin to trust that he is always there for you and that he made you unique and wonderful…you can turn each day into a chance to discover more about yourself, the God who loves you, and what fills you with deep joy.

I want to immerse myself in the joy that comes from you, God. I want to be surrounded by it, filled with it, and eager to share it with others. Discovering more about my unique self and purpose in you replenishes my spirit, my hope, and my faith.

Character

Words for Character

I know, my God, that you test the
heart and are pleased with integrity.
All these things have I given
willingly and with honest intent.

1 Chronicles 29:17

My soul clings to you;
your right hand upholds me.

Psalm 63:8

The Lord will keep you from all harm—
he will watch over your life;
the Lord will watch over
your coming and going
both now and forevermore.

Psalm 121:7-8

Then you will understand
what is right and just
and fair—every good path.
For wisdom will enter your heart,
and knowledge will be
pleasant to your soul.

PROVERBS 2:9-10

———

Where, then, is boasting? It is excluded.
On what principle? On that of observing
the law? No, but on that of faith. For
we maintain that a man is justified by
faith apart from observing the law.

ROMANS 3:27-28

———

Each man should give what he has decided
in his heart to give, not reluctantly or under
compulsion, for God loves a cheerful giver.

2 CORINTHIANS 9:7

———

Keeping It Equal

I want to believe that if I have more wealth, more security, and more of the world's foundation beneath my feet…I will be a better person. I'll serve God enthusiastically. My thoughts will quickly turn to the needy. I'll be generous in heart and spirit. Yet, I know that having more does not lead to more generosity, integrity, and service.

With more money comes more responsibility, obligation, and pressure. That's the formula of the world. God's formula for a good life is to give more than we have. To give freely of our heart, our service, our devotion, and our compassion no matter our earnings. In fact, your net worth is totally unrelated to your actual worth. Let that truth shape your character and how you spend your heart.

Can I help it if I want the security of the world? It is hard to let go of that. It is all that I see around me. Your ways can feel distant, God. Direct my eyes to all that you are and all that I am supposed to become. Let these define me. Lead me not to security but to generosity of heart and blessing.

You Tell Me

I wait and I wait for an answer sometimes. I pray for it. I watch for it. I ask others to pray for it and watch for it. I tap my toes. I count the ceiling tiles. I watch seasons come and go. I know there are lessons during this seeming interlude. Who am I when I'm not given what I demand right away? Who am I when I'm dependent on God completely?

It would be nice if we always had certainty about God's will and next step for us. But then we wouldn't have the wisdom that does come during the waiting and the watching. We are being shaped with great precision during those times. Don't miss it.

———◆———

I am waiting, Lord. You are probably waiting as well...for me to grow a little, rest a little, settle into contentment for once in my life, and to trust you completely. Waiting used to seem like a waste; now I know that it was my misuse of the waiting that has been wasteful. Forgive me, and help me trust.

Deal or No Deal

What temptations cause you to undermine your values, your measures of decency? Are you solid in a sense of self and faith until you face off with a particular roadblock? Sex, gambling, money, anger, impatience, greed, insecurity, competition, judgment? It feels good to rule out a few of these with a clear "Oh, I never struggle with *that!*" But there are probably a few on this list or in your life that are a constant struggle.

Think through the sins, the temptations that put your sanity and purpose at risk. We all have points of weakness, but what we do with them determines our spiritual health and recovery. Give them each, one by one, over to God in prayer regularly. Confronting such problems means you are regaining strength over them, by the grace of God.

That bad habit of mine…the rationalizing…it has to go. God help me when I start making deals with my integrity, my dreams, my beliefs. When I look at my life and my troubles, I see a list of reoccurring struggles. May I relinquish control of all these areas to your world-creating, future-shaping power!

Caving In (It Can Be Good)

Have you ever strongly felt the urge to do something because it was right or loving or necessary…and yet you wanted to fight it off? I have. I worry if I give myself over to the still small voice of God, I'll lose my own voice. I worry that this one step will turn into one hundred more, and I just don't have that kind of energy.

When we feel that urge toward goodness, wholeness, service, hospitality, or kindness, none of the worries matter. Really. Take the plunge. Cave in to conscience, give in to God's leading, and dive in to divine intervention. This is not only freeing, it is the beginning of all-out faithful living.

---

*Break down the barriers to my heart. Lead me
to let go of my hang-ups so that I can reach out
to others when the time is right. When I try to let
myself off the hook because I am busy or uncertain,
remind me that my life is bigger than I am.
Remind me that you have plans beyond my own.*

It's the Little Things

The other day I made a really good choice. I knew I wouldn't see the end result. And I had to sacrifice something I cared about. I know, it isn't about me; but the truth is that I was elated. All day I felt good about the chance to make something right in the world. It was God who made it happen, but I was a part of it. I asked God to use me and he did.

We have many opportunities to serve this world and the God who made it. Don't wait for grand gestures. Stop where you are right now. Grab on to the opportunity in front of you.

---

*Open my eyes to the little things today. Reveal to
me the ways that my attitude and my behavior
and my choices can serve you and your children.*

Great Intentions

I mean to do well. Don't we all? We wake up, set out for the day, and have every intention of making it through with a bit of integrity and grace. Do you stumble as much as I do? Do you not even notice until the mishap has happened, the hurtful action has injured another, or the misstep trampled all over someone's feelings?

Often our first response is really our very human response that is shaped by fatigue, anger, envy, or shortsightedness. Turn good intentions into God's intended wisdom for your steps, decisions, and responses.

---

*God, protect others from my times of weakness when
I say words that can hurt their feelings. Help me
hold my tongue before I unleash my problems, my
issues, my fears on some undeserving soul! Lord,
I want to keep my intentions pure and right.*

Needy and in Need

To be deemed clingy in our society is to be considered a failure, a person who requires the endless support, energy, and pity of others. But in spiritual terms, clinging to God and his power is a sign of strength. It does the soul well to reach out to God in total dependence. Only then are we drawing our identity from the one true power.

The undesirable form of neediness is born of many unmet, buried, real needs; don't hold back from connecting to God or to those he gives you who can offer friendship, support, and guidance. You are made to need God's mercy and wisdom.

—◆—

I resist being dependent upon you, God. I've tried to go it alone for a long time. But life is giving me cause to reevaluate this stance. I need you. There it is. I need you and your strength and your salvation and your mercy.

Glad Someone Notices

There is much I like to hide about my life. I don't tell others about my eating habits, the thoughts I harbor, the moments when anger consumes me, or the way I space off when I should be working. But as ashamed as I am of these and other indiscretions, there is a part of me that is very thankful that God sees my comings and my goings; he witnesses my heart in its goodness and stubbornness. And he still loves me.

There is freedom in having accountability to your Maker. There is such sweetness in God's grace, but first we must surrender the good, the bad, the semicrazy, and the mistakes. At the end of the day you will be glad that someone noticed you...all of you.

The shelter of your love protects me. You know all and see all. I am continuously amazed that you do not reject me for my past mistakes and current fumblings. You teach me and lead me, and you care about the person I become. Thank you for seeing all of me.

Big Head

Do we really think we understand the mechanics of life, biology, spirituality, purpose, or relationship better than the One who made them? I confess some days I actually *do*. Conceit inflates my false sense of security like a rubber raft setting sail for the New World (where I am the leader, of course). And like most overused inflatable items, my ego is destined for a leak, a pop, or a slow fizzle into nothing more than apologies and humiliation.

God desires to see us through to purpose, fulfillment, and knowledge. We just have to learn to seek godly actions instead of I-am-God delusions.

Yep. I do think I know best a lot of times, even though my track record would prove otherwise. I'm stubborn, God. I believe in you, but I let my agenda and ego take over. Let my recent mistakes be gentle reminders of how fallible my judgment can be and how enormous my need for you is.

What Is Left?

After hardship comes and goes, after moods swing us from here to there, after sugar highs turn to lows, we are left with ourselves—the tears, fears, successes, joys, and dreams. And there's more. Beyond these we can discover even more about ourselves. When we look at our identity as a child of God, our true core is witnessed.

See the you God is proud of. See the you God leads through a life patterned after no other. When emotions and aspirations fade, the truth of who you are in God radiates.

<hr />

I've had my share of highs and lows. I realize how my mood and my sense of value impacts my response to circumstances when I should be turning to my faith response. Guide me to rely on your love and instruction as my foundation for all that I do and all that I am.

Peace and Security

Words for Peace and Security

Not one of all the LORD's good
promises to the house of Israel
failed; every one was fulfilled.

JOSHUA 21:45

———◆———

I will establish my covenant with you, and
you will know that I am the LORD.

EZEKIEL 16:62

———◆———

I say to you: Ask and it will be given to you;
seek and you will find; knock and the door
will be opened to you. For everyone who
asks receives; he who seeks finds; and to
him who knocks, the door will be opened.

LUKE 11:9-10

———◆———

I will do whatever you ask in my name, so
that the Son may bring glory to the Father.

JOHN 14:13

———◆———

This is the covenant I will make with them
after that time, says the Lord.
I will put my laws in their hearts, and
I will write them on their minds.

HEBREWS 10:16

———✦———

Because God wanted to make the
unchanging nature of his purpose very
clear to the heirs of what was promised,
he confirmed it with an oath. God did
this so that, by two unchangeable things
in which it is impossible for God to lie,
we who have fled to take hold of the hope
offered to us may be greatly encouraged.

HEBREWS 6:17-18

———✦———

Let us hold unswervingly to the hope we
profess, for he who promised is faithful.

HEBREWS 10:23

———✦———

Pinky Swear

As kids, when someone made a promise, we liked to require lots of pomp and circumstance to make sure our bases were covered—a pinky swear, a handshake, a vow to sacrifice a favorite toy should the friend waiver in her commitment.

The difference between our version of promise and God's version is that his covenant is unshakable and eternal. Our actions don't change the solidity of his promises. He doesn't spit on his palm and ask for a high five, nor does he ask us to perform. The only ritual involved is the one of belief. If you are rusty on this, follow me. Lean into his love gently, faithfully, completely. You're covered.

I'm sorry for the times that I expect you to jump through hoops in order to satisfy my human version of promise. The truth is, I want to be freed from this way of thinking. Each day that I spend in your faithful presence leads me from doubt to belief. And your unconditional love covers me.

Right There

While paying for a DVD at a kiosk, I became aware of a person standing very close. My first feelings were (1) worry that my debit-card info was visible and (2) polite concern that I was making someone wait. When I turned to leave, I saw a tall, young woman who didn't look hurried or as if she were committing my PIN to memory.

When my awareness of God's presence is heightened, my first responses are similar. Either I'm afraid God will see my guarded secrets, or I'm concerned that God is tired of waiting for me to grow in faith. Eventually it sinks in…that despite what we've done or what we haven't done, God remains. And when we feel the spirit of fear come over us, all we have to do is look over our shoulder and remember that God is with us.

---

*Release me from my worries about your getting
too close, God. When I feel your presence, I want
to rejoice in this security. Let me rest in your
omnipresence and your grace. You are with me.
I pray to realize what a gift this is every day.*

Promises, Promises

Promises fall loosely from my lips when I'm in a hurry to discuss other important matters, like the length of my to-do list. Later, I end up digging through the debris of broken promises. My purpose then becomes more about damage control than living abundantly.

When we honor our commitments to others, to stewardship, to servanthood, to integrity, we can live with freedom and joy. May we pray for discernment before we speak promises. And when we indulge in one of the most popular sins of our times—overextending ourselves to the point of ineffectiveness—may we learn to ask for help.

⬧

*God, silence my tongue if I am about to make a
promise I cannot keep. Allow me to understand what
I can take on and what I cannot. Grant me wisdom
so that I may avoid the debris of my mistakes. Give
me strength to be a person of honor. I long to model
your eternal promises by the way I live this life.*

Strong Finish

I'm in a recovery leg of my journey. My pace is slow, and I am trying to gather and conserve energy for the race I know will kick in up ahead. In the past, I mistook these times as moments of weakness or failure, but God intends for us to refuel. God wants us to lean on his might so that we are prepared and encouraged.

When you feel unable to keep going, you are ready for the recovery leg. In fact, most of us are well beyond ready before we realize God's desire to carry, direct, and renew us. God wants you to finish strong; he just didn't intend for you to run alone.

———————

Lead me on, God. I am weary. I am tired. I find myself stumbling often. Forgive me for refusing to trust your strength early on. I wanted to run on my own terms. With each step, I'm learning how to give my pace over to your peace and my race over to your restoration.

Tell Me More

I like to know that happy times are happening and that people are achieving goals, finding joy, and reaching for their personal callings. When I read of someone's taking a leap of faith, my heart rises with the arc of the story and beats with possibility. Don't we all want these bits of inspiration?

When we catch ourselves listening more carefully to our inner voices of doubt than to God's steady words of encouragement, it is time to ask for a new way to hear his promises. God gives us many stories of good news and is the author of *the* good news. Are you ready to listen?

Tell me more about the goodness of your will and your ways. Give me an ear for all that is wise and worthy. May I ignore that which is false, harmful, and unrighteous. Where I have become lazy in my quest for honor and honesty, inspire me with role models. Give me the courage to stand strong so that my life declares your good news.

Wishes and Dreams

I've closed my eyes to blow out many candles and have made many wishes. Those wishes became dreams; some eventually turned into the stepping stones of goals. I walk forward with my sights set on how I'd like life to be.

Our wishes and dreams are important. They often rise up to lead us toward our true calling and purpose. But when our hope is grounded in the security of God's faithfulness, we can do more than make a wish, we can lift up a prayer and know that it is heard.

—◆—

God, reveal to me those dreams that are of your plan and purpose for me. Thank you for those moments when I feel the wonder of a future hope. I know that the wishes that do come true are reflections of your brilliant life-giving light.

This Life Protected By...

I house-sat for a friend who had a security system. I'm used to just unlocking a dead bolt, so I was a little flustered when I had to enter a series of numbers quickly. If I was off by one digit or reversed the order or paused too long between entries, an alarm sounded.

We can be thankful that God does not require such precise steps in order to gain entrance to his presence and protection. When we are his, we can rest in the security of his shelter—no passcode needed. If we are unable to connect with God, it is time to look at what personally keeps us from entering his presence. The door is open.

Thank you, thank you for being so accessible.
My heart had high walls built around it until
you showed me the comfort and character of
unconditional love. I can stop protecting my
heart because you are there to watch over me.

Take a Vow

Your soul experiences a supernatural joy when the vow of faith is taken. It makes you want to stand before friends, family, and strangers and declare your undying love for never-ending Love. You'll find yourself looking for ways to show and tell others "I love because he first loved me."

Committed faith calls you to move, speak, and act out of gratitude. Your sorrows and celebrations are shaped by the very moment you took your vow and left solitary struggle in exchange for a life connected to and shared by God. The rewards of a shared life await you.

I commit to so many people, obligations, and even struggles. Lead me to the altar of renewed faith commitment. I want to know you personally, intimately, and completely. Thank you for not only promising a forever I can believe in, but also walking with me from this day forward.

Searching

Shelves of knickknacks overflowed. I kept walking. Delicate jewelry sparkled beneath the glass of a display case. I moved on. Candles in shades of autumn gave off scents of a Thanksgiving feast. I continued my search. An unassuming tray of charms featuring words of inspiration rested on the counter. "That's it!" I said and purchased several treasures for my friend.

If you have times when you feel like you are wandering through life, your desire to find God's best will lead you. Even when you don't know what you're searching for, the treasures you'll discover will be just what you need, long for, and are made for.

———◆———

I shouldn't be surprised by the many moments,
connections, and wonders you bring into my life,
but I am. May I never get so lost in my search
that I don't notice the treasures that are of your
purpose for me. When I say, "That's it!" after a
long time of unknowing, may I give thanks.

Unchanging

A friend I haven't seen in a long time e-mailed me to share that he had a dream in which I had dyed my hair a different color. In the dream he was trying to tell me nicely that even though I looked good in my new, interesting style, I shouldn't try to be like anyone else.

The details of the dream weren't accurate, but the essence was important. It is tempting to want to emulate a style, goal, or vision for life that we have witnessed in another. But God doesn't call us to be like someone else; he calls us to become who we are intended to be. Our preferences may come and go, but our identity in Christ is unchanging.

———◆———

*Lord, how am I trying to be someone that I am not?
How have I wasted vital energy on trying to change
myself in superficial ways? You do not call me to change
who I am; you call me to the great I AM and promise
transformation through your grace and mercy. When
I stray, allow me to protect the me that is your child.*

Grace

Words for Grace

When [Barnabas] arrived and saw the
evidence of the grace of God, he was
glad and encouraged them all to remain
true to the Lord with all their hearts.

ACTS 11:23

Now I commit you to God and to the
word of his grace, which can build
you up and give you an inheritance
among all those who are sanctified.

ACTS 20:32

Where sin increased, grace
increased all the more.

ROMANS 5:20

By the grace God has given me, I laid
a foundation as an expert builder, and
someone else is building on it.

1 CORINTHIANS 3:10

By the grace of God I am what I am, and
his grace to me was not without effect. No,
I worked harder than all of them—yet not
I, but the grace of God that was with me.

1 CORINTHIANS 15:10

All this is for your benefit, so that the grace that
is reaching more and more people may cause
thanksgiving to overflow to the glory of God.

2 CORINTHIANS 4:15

Just as you excel in everything—in faith,
in speech, in knowledge, in complete
earnestness and in your love for us—see
that you also excel in this grace of giving.

2 CORINTHIANS 8:7

And God is able to make all grace
abound to you, so that in all things at
all times, having all that you need, you
will abound in every good work.

2 CORINTHIANS 9:8

Witness

We are witnesses to God's love and grace daily. Let's grab on to these confirmations of all that our Creator is and will be for us and for the world. When we are exposed to bad news or we find ourselves serving a slice of gossip or believing a rumor, it also becomes our opportunity to go the way of goodness—to listen only to the still small voice that clearly guides us with truth.

Grace happens minute by minute. If you are not seeing it in action throughout your day, then it is time to put it into practice. Share with others the great gift you experience as a child of God.

———◆———

In many ways you reveal your sweet forgiveness
and power to make the broken whole. Help me
to express your love through kindness, justice,
compassion, purity, and the willingness to
be a reflection of your abundant grace.

Foundation of Grace

Grace—how can something that sounds so soft, comfortable, and giving be so solid? When people engage in the details of dogma or the arguments of theology, I find the interaction initially exciting and motivating. I want to understand God and faith in deeper ways. But after a while, debates make me dizzy. I want to lie down on something solid.

Ah, back to grace. It is my truth and hope and belief. My life has been wrapped in it, covered by it, and restored because of it. When I stand firmly on the rock of grace, the questions can keep coming, but I rest in what I know to be true.

Opinions, public forum, and issue debates help me
define my faith in stronger terms and convictions.
But, God, I'm so thankful that I can take refuge
in your grace. When I face doubts or questions
or even my own curiosity, I know that I stand
firm on a foundation of your good grace.

Portion Control

We live in a world caught between a sense of super-sized entitlement and a belief in repentance via portion control. The view of grace can be similar. Some view it as an open-ended license to do as they please. Others view it as a restricted blessing distributed based on merit. Either image distorts the beauty of God's great grace.

There is no human-crafted formula that will figure out how grace works, how it covers hurts and sins and shattered hearts. God's grace has us covered in proportion to what we need. As consumers, we can ask how much is too much. As Christians we need only say "Your grace is sufficient" and "Thank you" on our way to a richer, deeper faith.

I'm sorry for the times I acted as though your grace was there for me as backup so that I could do what I wanted. I don't want to take it for granted. I want to experience the beauty, the depth, the joy, and the miracle of the grace gift.

Pass It Along

We are so fortunate to know grace firsthand, but it isn't meant to stop with us. Try committing a week of passing grace on to others. Anyone and everyone. The slow clerk at the market, the lost driver who keeps veering, the friend who is worried about the same thing yet again, the family member quick with hurtful comments, the child who makes mistakes. Show them grace by responding with patience, understanding, and empathy.

Experience grace from God. Model it for others. And extend it to yourself. We can be so tough and critical when it comes to our own looks, choices, gifts, and efforts. View your life through the forgiving lens of grace, and every situation will look fresh and optimistic.

———❖———

I stand in your forgiveness and mercy each day, but I forget to share this freedom with others through my actions and responses. Remind me of the times I have received grace from friends and family and strangers. I know that I can become self-focused all day long. Turn my attention to the grace that abounds, and may I be a part of it today.

God Doesn't Leave

I've had friends float in and out of my life. I've lost loved ones either through death or distance. Some relationships were harder to let go of than others, because the void made me feel alone. It isn't easy to be left out or left behind. We learn this early on in the politics of playgrounds.

When the heart feels abandoned and hope bends from the weight of loneliness, we can turn our worried faces toward God. We can cling to his hem and hold tightly. When our tears are brushed away by fingers of compassion and our shoulders lovingly patted by the hands that shaped our lives, we know that Grace never leaves us behind.

❖

I want to get lost in the folds of unconditional love and unrestricted comfort. You don't ask why I'm so upset. You've witnessed my hurt, my loss, and my silly woes. You never judge the importance of what I bring to you. It all matters. Besides, you know that I am here today to remind myself that you are here always.

When Things Aren't Things

If we keep the harvest of faith such as grace, love, compassion, kindness, etc. as lofty by-products of belief, we miss the chance to express them tangibly. We let ourselves off the hook of an active faith. Faith without works is saved by grace, but it becomes a lifeless faith and ends up looking far different from the image of God.

Dig into grace, love, compassion, kindness, and forgiveness, and pull out something that the world or even one single person can relate to. Give these blessings dimension and weight. How? Share a meal. Make a donation. Take the hand of someone who needs healing. Give away some "thing" that matters to you. Help load groceries for a fragile stranger. Things are so much more than things when they are used to express a living, active, abundant faith.

———◆———

What is right in front of me that I need to fix, give away, pass along, lift up, release, or transform into something useful? How can my hands serve today? How can my strength bring relief to someone? What can I give that is indeed sacrifice so that my discomfort is turned into the comfort of another? Help me give my faith a workout.

Wantin' Ways

When we see the even better version of the techno-gadget we just bought, it is difficult but important to remember that our truest wants are met by God's grace alone—if we'll release them, that is! As tightly as we hold on to the material world as our source of identity and power, we are to hold on to God's truth and purpose for us.

The more we let go, the more grace abounds. The more we step out in faith without the safety net of résumé success, the more we sense the power of grace. Our eyes might wander to the next big thing, but may our hearts look upward at the one true thing.

———◆———

*It is by your grace that I move forward, feel
love, experience blessing, survive trials, and
see beyond doubt to hope. My false needs come
and go as quickly as commercials, but my
authentic, life-transforming longings will only
be filled by the bounty of a faithful heart.*

The Way It Should Be

My tribute to God goes a bit like this: "I falter. You recover. I betray good intentions. You redeem hearts. I fear. You calm. I give up. You show me the way. I distrust. You remain. I cheat. You offer real answers. I backpedal. You inspire me to press on."

Do you have a similar ongoing pattern? Did you know that this is a good thing? We have every opportunity to try, to dare, to live fully because when our shortcomings are strongest or our need for extra help the greatest, God's power is at work and on display in our lives. We are walking, talking billboards for God's grace and hope. Repeat after me, "I am weak, but you are strong." Yes, Jesus loves us…and may the world know it.

When I credit you with my life and life's strength, others will see your glory in my missteps or my victories. I need not worry about the outcome because you are shaping it carefully. I want people to know that I am weak but you are strong.

Testify

If we understand what faith is all about, we will become expert witnesses to God's grace. When we get that it is not our strength but God's that ushers us through each day, then we can speak of this truth in the court of everyday people. Whether we're with those who know or don't know God, our offerings of faith, encouragement, God's peace, and wisdom should not vary.

Life is hard. Let's face it. But let's face it by walking faithfully. And when we do, there will be no other explanation for why we are content, sane, kind, whole, forgiving, trusting, and eager to testify as an eyewitness to grace.

God, I have hesitated to share what I know with others. I don't trust myself to get it right or to reflect you sufficiently. How can I...I am only me? But you don't need me to fix everything or every person I encounter. You call me to the stand to share my story, my version of one life dependent on grace. This I can do...with your help, of course.

Back to Freedom

I've grown accustomed to fallback sources of freedom that come with worldly credentials: power, financing, might, escape, approval, security of the masses. I want them backing my every move, because what if life doesn't turn out the way I planned? What if there's illness? What if there's loss of work? What if there's war? What if there are unknowns?

Every time we greet the sun and step into a new day, there are unknowns. But when we lean into the certainty of our all-knowing God, we rest in absolute freedom.

---

*Life can feel like a free fall. Help me release
my grip on the world's securities so that I look
only to the safety net of grace. You don't keep me
from the "what ifs," but when I listen to your
leading, you guide me through the unknowns.*

Direction

Words for Direction

Direct me in the path of your commands,
for there I find delight.

PSALM 119:35

You guide me with your counsel,
and afterward you will take me into glory.

PSALM 73:24

Show me your ways, O LORD,
teach me your paths;
guide me in your truth and teach me,
for you are God my Savior,
and my hope is in you all day long.

PSALM 25:4-5

Into your hands I commit my spirit;
redeem me, O LORD, the God of truth.

PSALM 31:5

Teach me your way, O LORD;
lead me in a straight path.

PSALM 27:11

The path of life leads upward for the wise.

PROVERBS 15:24

Open Eyes

Some days I feel like I am sleepwalking. A haze clouds my mind and heart as I make my way through the maze of scheduled tasks or conversations. And then a comment, a thought, or a scene will capture my attention. I've been missing out on the gift of a new day, a series of possibilities, and a string of moments that God designed for me to experience, to witness, and to hold in heart and mind.

Some "pay attention" moments might be deemed unremarkable by others, but to me they are windows into God's heart for my life. I see his humor in a child's silly joke, his wisdom in a friend's counsel, and his love for me when I come across a well-timed verse from Scripture that speaks to my immediate situation.

Pull me out of the fog of routine so I can witness the wonders that I used to pass by on my way to more busyness. Open my eyes to every moment. Allow me to see the people and the possibilities and the path you carve out for me each day.

In Charge

With my cell phone on, my e-mail filling the screen, and my mental list of duties for the day, I feel slightly powerful. I'm in charge of the moment and, if I stay on task, maybe even in control of the day.

The world would have us think we are in control of our days and our lives. It becomes easy to think of God as a good friend rather than the all-knowing Creator who sees and shapes the big picture and the fine details. Eventually interruptions and disconnections change the course of even the best plans. Consider these disruptions blessings—gentle reminders that we're not in charge but are loved, noticed, and guided by the One who is.

You are my only power source. You made me so that I could use my abilities, my mind, and my life to bring you glory. When I start to think that I control people, details, and my future, remind me—gently please— that I'm not in charge of life. I'm in your charge.

Formula

Most parents wish their children came with a manual. For our own lives, we know that's ridiculous thinking…yet how many of us are secretly hoping that we'll come upon a formula for success and happiness?

There isn't a secret code that will fulfill the universal quest for significance. You personally *know* the Maker of mankind, the Genius behind gravity, and the Inventor of starfish and eyelashes; the only formula you need is: one (you) + one (God) equals relationship. Profound and simple—these are the characteristics of a great truth.

Okay, I'll confess that I've been hoping that formula would appear. I was trying to figure out my life without the power of faith. I got caught up in human answers. God, protect me from my own desires so that I can rest in your desires for me.

Awake and Alive

How often do we live our lives without watching for glimpses of God and his wonders? When we place our feet on the floor and begin a new day with a stretch, let's add in a short prayer to be fully aware of the One who is fully alive and in charge and in love with life. Let this prayer shape our day, our mood, our outlook, and our hope.

Let's awaken our hearts, minds, and spirits so that we don't waste the sacred gift of a day. Even a regular day has its miracle moments, if we'll just open our eyes in time to be a witness to the life God is shaping for us, in us, around us, and through us daily.

———

*Creator, show me what it is to be among the fully
awake, the fully vested, the fully living. Release
me from the numbness of routine, and recharge
my spirit with your love. I want to see your beauty
and purpose and power in this life I live.*

Typecasting

Am I an introvert or an extrovert? Do I lean toward type-A personality characteristics? Do I have the "it" factor? Am I more of a behind-the-scenes person or a leader? What credentials do I bring to the table? The answers to the questions aren't about who I am; they are about finding a label that the world can use for quick acceptance or dismissal.

Thank goodness God doesn't try to force us into stereotypes. He's the Maker of the individual. There is, however, a label worth aspiring to—child of God—and it requires only that we become the one of a kind he created us to be.

God, I know you have great plans for me and provide me with what I need. Teach me to stop trying to fit into the world's categories when I can stand with courage and confidence in the identity and faith you blessed me with even before I was born.

Cliffhanger

Purpose is like a huge canyon. Something one could get lost in, fall into, or spend many hours staring at with amazement and uncertainty. Are we meant to just get to the other side? Should we repel down to the canyon floor? If we started out in the wrong direction on a shaky overhang, would someone pull us back to safety?

Even if we don't personally ask "What is my purpose here in this life?" we are still reminded of the question by our fellow journey travelers. The good news is that we aren't standing here alone. God is our guide into it, through it, or around it—depending on our particular purpose. (And for the record, he will pull you back to safety.)

❖

So many unanswered questions. I want to know my purpose. I want to stand at the edge of the canyon and feel freedom rather than fear, possibility rather than panic, direction rather than danger. I might close my eyes sometimes, but I'm ready, God. Lead me to it.

Keep Walking

When the path gets rocky, remain steady. When the hills become steep, start climbing. When bystanders question your direction, stay the course. When bumps feel like mountains, step higher. When you are thirsty and hungry, watch for sustenance. When you are lonely and doubting, ask for help. When your body aches, lean on the strength of the Spirit. When the road is cast in darkness, shed light on it.

When you look behind you and don't recognize the path and you look ahead and it, too, is foreign, keep walking. You're almost there.

God, there are so many unknowns. I'd love to step onto a path and know without a doubt that there's not any other way to go. I'm absolutely right. Instead, the faith journey requires me to give my path over to you and know that you are God. The way of truth. The way of life. The way of love. And the way I should go. Absolutely.

So Very Green

That grass over there is lush, thick, and glossy, and the green is so deep it bears a halo of blue. My friend's gifts and abilities are so colorful and remarkable I can't help but stare at his journey and question why I didn't follow a similar route. Sure, my gifts are completely different, and yes I'd have to give up my passions to follow his, but still…

Here's the truth: the grass is always going to seem greener on the other side. But it really is all about the lighting. When you illuminate your own portion of purpose, it is brilliant too. Spend time observing it and being grateful. It's quite incredible on your side of life.

Why has it taken me so long to see the beauty of my own life? I've taken for granted those strengths you have given me. I've squandered time and my resources by ignoring your leading. I'm ready to celebrate the wonder of this life you have entrusted to me. I return it to you and ask to be a part of the miracle.

Test Kitchen

All the cooking shows these days remind us how the wonders of a good meal represent those of a good life. It's about the pleasure of the senses, the ingredients that make the ordinary sumptuous, and the opportunity of creating something worth savoring.

Go to the test kitchen for your life. Add inspired ingredients for new flavor like new friends, adventure, trying a hobby, trust in yourself, new perspective about your job, whatever has been missing in your batches. A sprinkle of possibility, a dash of insight, and a cup of faith mixed with plenty of prayer—a life of meaning is in the works!

<hr />

Your love is poured out over my life. I want to serve you by making the most of my days. I know that there are many ingredients you've brought my way that I've been reluctant to try. I don't want to be afraid to add richness. I want to savor every moment.

Healing

Words for Healing

Jacob made a vow, saying, "If God will
be with me and will watch over me on
this journey I am taking and will give
me food to eat and clothes to wear so
that I return safely to my father's house,
then the LORD will be my God."

GENESIS 28:20-21

————✦————

O LORD my God, I called to you for help
and you healed me.

PSALM 30:2

————✦————

Rise up and help us;
redeem us because of your unfailing love.

PSALM 44:26

————✦————

Restore us, O God;
make your face shine upon us,
that we may be saved.

PSALM 80:3

⁘

The LORD protects the simplehearted;
when I was in great need, he saved me.

PSALM 116:6

⁘

Pleasant words are a honeycomb,
sweet to the soul and healing to the bones.

PROVERBS 16:24

⁘

Heal me, O LORD, and I will be healed;
save me and I will be saved,
for you are the one I praise.

JEREMIAH 17:14

⁘

Be Here

I've been asking God to be with me a lot lately, to wrap me in his full presence, and to help me feel closer to normal. I want healing from soul to bone, from mind to skin, from prayer to truth. My focus on this is all-consuming.

Thirst for mercy comes on so violently when want and worry leave us stripped of all other resources. God must wish we'd seek to be filled and satiated before we stand in drought's ruin. Go to his mercy today. Give yourself over to God as a daily practice and preserve the reserve of your soul's only source of renewal.

I want to mend the parched places of my mind and spirit on my own terms or at least when it is more convenient. Today I come to you with the hurts I recognize and those I have ignored. May your mercy rush over me, and may it bring healing.

On the Bridge

From brokenness to wholeness is a great distance. I've stood here before, but this time it is more daunting. Honestly, I can't even see what this situation looks like on the other side of pain. What if there is a drop-off somewhere between hurt and healing? A jagged cliff where one false hope can leave me tumbling?

When we face the chasm of illness or failing or despair, the restoration might not always be visible, but God's hope, grace, mercy, faithfulness, and love are shaping it even now. When the abyss is vast, God's bridge of healing is rising up. Take a step forward; it will hold you up.

———◆———

I'm afraid to step forward in this experience. I can't manage the unknown without the assurance of your presence. Your healing does not require me to "manage" anything. I know this too. Help me release this desire to control every detail, Lord. I'd rather walk with faith, even into the unknown, than without it.

Sutures

When we walk through trials, the stings and the pains we feel might seem familiar. We might be facing a different hardship, but wounds from long ago can be reopened if we haven't given them over to God's healing. When we nurse them with our own version of healing—self-help solutions, a change of job or address, burying the pain—we will feel the pain afresh eventually.

God takes our emotional and spiritual injuries and seals them with sutures of promise, mercy, and understanding. Exchange your version of remedy for God's authentic healing.

———————

I hurt so deeply. I keep revisiting this pain. Each time, I think I have suffered a different wound caused by a new weapon. But this one is not new for me. I've kept it open and buried by my ignorance and stubbornness. Mend me, Lord. I want true healing.

Soul Shattering

Like a lip quivering, the soul expresses the first tremors of fear. What is shaking the foundation you have built your security on? Is it a loss of a loved one? An uncertain prognosis in life or health? A crisis of faith? An unexplainable fear that takes over?

Sometimes we don't know what causes our souls to shatter. It might not be for you to ever discover—that is a difficult truth to accept. But hold tightly to the peace of what you do know…*who* will put the pieces back together. And he will.

God, I can't stop shaking on the inside. I want to feel whole and complete. Take the fragments of my spirit and piece me together in your time and in your grace. May I stand on the unshakable ground of hope so that the world can see your strength.

Eyes on Jesus

I've been waiting for healing so long that I've started to watch for something else. Any distraction will do. Like an impatient tourist on my way to a paradise, I begin to think the desolate stops on the way represent the destination, and I become discouraged.

The wonder of the destination will be lost on us if we don't realize the meaning of each time of waiting. When the view is dismal, it is because we have missed the point of the stop—it is a time to focus our eyes ever so closely on Jesus.

———

This time has a purpose in my life. I am thankful that it causes me, compels me, to seek out your face. There is peace and comfort in that face. Love cradles me even when I am resistant. Beauty envelops me even when the view is not what I signed up to see. Don't let me be tempted by distraction when your beauty is so clearly what I am meant to notice.

Better than New

Americans are obsessed with overhauling houses, bodies, cars, and lives. If we had enough money or the right opportunity, wouldn't we all love a makeover of some kind? Why then do we often deny the freely given transformations of faith—from damaged to mended, from dead to living, from ignorant to wise, from blind to sighted?

Maybe our vision of remodel is far too limited. We want a new look, a new ride, or a new size. God is ready to give us a better-than-new life. What are we waiting for?

———◆———

I've been longing for a touch-up when you are offering a complete exchange of old for new. I carry around sins, hurts, regrets, and shame while wishing for a house with a swimming pool. God, help me grow up so that I can experience a life, a purpose, a faith that is better than new.

God Only Knows

When nobody is watching, God is there. When you have been abandoned, cut by words, torn by abuse…God sees it, and he weeps for the loss of justice, innocence, and peace. In the darkest moment, you are not left to bear the suffering alone.

God provides the strength you need right where you are. God has a plan in motion to repair your soul. He will bring you comfort, he will lead you to refuge, he will show you the tears he shed that moment when you thought you were lost forever.

❧

I am so thankful that I don't have to stand as a solo witness to the pain. I have been afraid to release the wound because I wanted there to be a record of the injustice and the reason for my brokenness. But you were there. You are here. And you share my sorrow because you love me. This love is the reason for my healing.

Over the Counter

Last year I had a sinus headache that turned to infection. However, I was busy with work, so I kept hoping an over-the-counter medication would correct the problem. Well, my real problem was my faulty thinking. One plane ride later, my head felt like it was in a vise, but my mind finally got the message: This problem isn't going away—get the antibiotics.

Have you ever done the same with a spiritual problem? Is there a reoccurring sin you try to fix with mere self-determination or positive thinking? It remains, doesn't it? And it causes more pain each time. Stop reaching for over-the-counter solutions when your painful sin needs super-natural healing.

———◆———

The pain is deep. My sin is beginning to consume me.
I wanted an easy out, and the truth is, you offer one.
You have offered to take this from me. My journey
won't be simple, but your answer is. Here. Take it.

What Can You Make of This?

Jigsaw puzzles may have caused a problem. They provide us with a finite number of pieces and a picture of the end result. With a little time and patience, everything comes together. But when it comes to pieces of our lives, the fragments that follow heartbreak or breakdowns, everything doesn't add up to the picture we have stuck in our heads.

This isn't about giving up, but giving *over*. Hand the pieces to God. He knows what the big picture looks like. Are you clutching a piece right now? Have you tried to force it to fit your image of healing? Let go. God is trying to make something wonderful.

❖

God, what can you make of all these pieces? I've been trying to force my emotions along so that I could say I was better. I wanted everyone around me to see the picture of someone who had moved past the pain. But I'm stuck, and I'm tired of this false image. I can't wait to see what you are going to make of this life of mine.

Compassion

Words for Compassion

You care for the land and water it;
you enrich it abundantly.
The streams of God are filled with water
to provide the people with grain,
for so you have ordained it.

PSALM 65:9

The LORD is gracious and compassionate,
slow to anger and rich in love.
The LORD is good to all;
he has compassion on all he has made.

PSALM 145:8-9

Do not judge, and you will not be
judged. Do not condemn, and you
will not be condemned. Forgive,
and you will be forgiven.

LUKE 6:37

Be kind and compassionate to one
another, forgiving each other, just
as in Christ God forgave you.

EPHESIANS 4:32

⁃◦◦◦⁃

As God's chosen people, holy and dearly
loved, clothe yourselves with compassion,
kindness, humility, gentleness and patience.

COLOSSIANS 3:12

⁃◦◦◦⁃

Finally, all of you, live in harmony with
one another; be sympathetic, love as
brothers, be compassionate and humble.

1 PETER 3:8

⁃◦◦◦⁃

Past Ourselves Is God

We try and try and try to make things right. And the next time our lives need fixing, we'll likely try again and stumble. I have news that I'm hoping you'll consider wonderfully freeing—we aren't meant to fix our own lives. When we fail at this task, there is a perfectly good reason. Or better said, there is a perfect God reason.

He is the perfecter of our lives and our faith. At the point where our ability ends, God awaits. Here we discover the significance of compassion—here we extend grace to ourselves as we fall into God's unconditional love.

When I say I'm done with trying, I mean it! Well, at least this time I mean it. I want to give over my circumstances to you so that I can personally, intimately experience the point where I end and you continue for eternity. I want to be free of my limitations.

Long Vision

"Jesus had compassion on them and touched their eyes. Immediately they received their sight and followed him" (Matthew 20:34). How has God healed you? How has his touch expanded your vision of life or love or purpose? When your eyes were opened to the resurrected life, did you immediately follow him?

The compassion of Christ changes everything—our view, our horizon, and our future. When we respond to the touch of healing with a desire to follow his ways of mercy, we will have our eyes opened to purpose and calling.

God, you have opened my eyes to your compassion,
to your promises, and to new life in you. I want
to leave behind the limited purpose I had been
walking in before my encounter with your saving
grace. Show me what is next. I am watching,
I am following, and I am believing.

Cultivating a Compassionate Life

It takes a lot of planning and care to grow a bountiful garden, which probably explains why I don't have one. How much more plotting and attention is required to nurture an abundant life! I can forego the backyard vegetables, but I long for a life that produces a good, decent harvest that honors God.

We know the Master Gardener, but we are also called to tend to our spiritual growth. One of the most important crops we can raise is that of compassion. The more you plant in the hearts of others, the more that will grow in your own life. It's plantin' season.

———◆———

Show me how to sow compassion. Alleviate my own anxieties and anger so that I can demonstrate your love to those I encounter—stranger or friend. My faith softens my heart; may this become the fertile ground in which compassion takes root.

Slow to Anger

There is no favoritism in God's kingdom. He is fond of all he has made. He has compassion and unconditional love for all his children. I love the idea of God being slow to anger and rich in love (Psalm 145:8-9). It is such an interesting pairing—anger and love; think how often we choose to express one over the other.

If we can adopt a "slow to anger" policy in our interactions, there will be a much better chance for love to take hold and shape our relationships.

I envision anger on one side of a seesaw and love on the other. God, how often do I try to sway a situation toward anger, when the shift should be toward your wealth of love? Don't let me slide toward indifference when a heart of compassion can anchor me to your faithfulness.

Empathize Me

Sympathy brings us flowers, it cries for us from a distance, and it keeps us in mind. But empathy sits with us in the sorrow or the difficulty. Empathy connects to the shared truth and questions in a person's journey. Empathy doesn't mind red eyes and messy hair and times of silence.

Being empathetic takes sacrifice. Often you must go to uncomfortable depths of your own spirit and sorrow to reach the source waters of empathy. But when you get there, you can draw from God's compassion, rest in uncertainty, and share the burden of another. When you get there, you get a glimpse of God's great love.

———◆———

Give me a heart beyond my own heart. I get too caught up in my opinions and my life circumstances. Still my thoughts, turn my focus to the deep need of another. Help me have patience to just sit with another person's pain…even when answers seem distant, even when it is uncomfortable.

Judge Not

I like to say that I am antijudgmental and pro-grace. Yet I still find this unattractive defense mechanism interfering with my days. I use judgment as a protective shield against the possible criticism of others—a first-strike strategy. "They can't hurt me because I can list five things wrong with them." No, this isn't logical, but it is human.

Judgment fills our thoughts quickly. It takes over our actions and responses. It leaves no room for understanding and compassion. It's helpful to have the image of a courtroom judge to associate with the word. Each time you judge another and place yourself above another child of God, you sentence that person and yourself to a life devoid of compassion.

❖

Lord, lead me away from the chambers of judgment.
When I get on my high horse and want to place
value on a person or their behavior, remind me
what I would be without you and your grace.
Fill my heart with unconditional compassion,
and help me leave the big judgments to you.

Compassion Sense

What's your style? Dramatic? Practical? Whimsical? Servanthood? Didn't you know there's a dress code for servanthood? Really, it's more of a uniform: "Clothe yourselves with compassion, kindness, humility, gentleness and patience" (Colossians 3:12).

Each day when you reach for the right attire, don't forget the spiritual clothing you'll need to love others, extend grace, be used by God, and get noticed for the statement you make by your faith accessories.

———◆———

I stand before you naked, my own nature stripped away so that I can be clothed by character that reflects you. You give us all unique personal styles through our own callings and purposes, and then you add to it with the fabric of compassion, kindness, humility, gentleness, and patience. May we wear it well.

Acts of Forgiveness

We've all seen the bumper stickers encouraging random acts of kindness. I'm thinking that maybe a better way to change the world would be through intentional acts of forgiveness. Our culture has become very blasé about the importance of asking for and extending forgiveness.

Think how your day and attitude would change if you started each morning with the intention of forgiving anyone and anything. Is your mind already drafting a list of things you couldn't possibly forgive? That's why this must be intentional. If we lean on our own measure of justice, we'll never adopt God's measure of grace. Go forth and forgive.

I forget to go to you with the burden of my sins and my weaknesses. It has been even longer since I asked another person for forgiveness, even though there have been many circumstances when it would've been the right thing. Lord, help me to step beyond my pride so that I can walk intentionally toward a life that gives and seeks forgiveness.

Tenderness

I used to watch my mother tenderize meat by pounding it or poking it with a fork. I must admit, I was a skeptic. Wouldn't such force harden the piece of beef or pork? But it always worked, and I became a believer (and a happy eater).

While many hearts have been hardened by the blows of disappointment, I would state the case for the power of trials and suffering to change the consistency of our hearts for the better. But only through God, and only with the power of prayer and grace. Our sadness and tough times can be transformed into tenderness and compassion. Become a believer.

———⚬———

God, I give you these hardened places of my spirit and mind. I've closed off my ability to nurture my wounds. They need the balm of your care. Tenderize my heart. Melt away the fear that keeps me from reaching out to others or from expressing my feelings. Please, Lord…turn this hardened life into one that can easily be shaped and seasoned by love.

From a Distance

Our computer home page reveals news and images of brutality, war, and pain. Some situations are far away, and that makes us feel a bit safer even if we are saddened by word of trouble for any nation, any people. We say "Isn't it a shame," or "God, do something!" but do we take on God's heart of compassion for these distant sorrows?

It's risky to move beyond a general concern to an involved compassion. You never know what God might call you to do should you invest your heart and prayers in the plight of another child of God. Remember, from where God is—in us and among us—the distance between you and them is nonexistent. Do something.

How can I help someone I don't know who is so far away? I know that you nudge me to begin with the person next to me. They have needs too. Yet what have I done to show them unconditional love? I will make the decision to stop passively viewing hardship so that I can begin living in an active state of compassion, for those near or far.

Fulfillment

Words for Fulfillment

From heaven the LORD looks down
and sees all mankind;
from his dwelling place he watches
all who live on earth—
he who forms the hearts of all,
who considers everything they do.

PSALM 33:13-15

How can I repay the LORD
for all his goodness to me?
I will lift up the cup of salvation
and call on the name of the LORD.
I will fulfill my vows to the LORD
in the presence of all his people.

PSALM 116:12-14

The LORD will fulfill [his purpose] for me;
your love, O LORD, endures forever—
do not abandon the works of your hands.

PSALM 138:8

When I fed them, they were satisfied;
when they were satisfied,
they became proud;
then they forgot me.

HOSEA 13:6

I always thank God for you because of
his grace given you in Christ Jesus. For
in him you have been enriched in every
way—in all your speaking and in all
your knowledge—because our testimony
about Christ was confirmed in you.

1 CORINTHIANS 1:4-6

God's Dependent

When we consider that God is our provider for *everything*, we also need to consider that we are dependent upon him for *everything*. If God had to file with the IRS, he'd do quite well. Each of us is a dependent living under his roof and relying on his care and feeding.

The truly amazing part is that our complete dependence on God is our pass to freedom and fulfillment. We can step forward without worries about our survival or purpose. These might still sneak into our thoughts, but we are free to let them go. You, me, our neighbors, our family members… we are listed under his charge.

Grant me dependence, Lord. That's right. I'm glad to be a dependent in your household. You care for me, you plot out my days, you deliver goodness to my doorstep, and you revive my soul. My hunger for a place in this world is fulfilled with the home of plenty in your heart.

It's Beyond Me

I've told God so many times that I am not up to the task of handling my current life stresses. I've expressed my anger about these pressures along with suggestions as to how they can be resolved. You see, I had plans, and this latest glitch was not in them. Have you ever had your perfect life plans interrupted?

I've figured out that this point of venting and possibly whining can be a good sign. It means we're finally getting close to the solution. When we get that life management is beyond our ability, then we're ready for God to take over. And do you know what? That life plan we had…it's nothing compared to what's in store for us with God at the helm.

❖

*God, lead me past this point. Beyond what I
can handle is the strength, your strength, that
I am supposed to rest in. Of course my life goes
haywire sometimes. It is because I was not created
to manage it on my own. Make this the life you
intended for me. I give it over to you completely.*

Satisfaction or Fulfillment

Do you look upon situations with a sense of satisfaction or dissatisfaction? Do people and results tend to disappoint you? What do you think you are waiting for to truly ease the void and the expectations? What blocks you from receiving joy and fulfillment? So many questions! But these do lead somewhere.

If you don't examine your barriers to an abundant life, it becomes easy to blame other people or God for your problems, worries, disappointments, and mistakes. I believe fulfillment comes only when we are faithful to truth. Discover what holds you back, and give that truth over to God. He transforms the fragments of disappointment into the whole of contentment.

❖

How long have I held back from a good, full life, Lord? I hold on to the failings of myself and those around me as an excuse. I lift them up and say, "See...this is all life is." But you take these and say they are not my truth, but they are the proof that I need you in order to be complete.

Zero-Interest Loan

Are you ever flat-out amazed at the life you're leading? Amazement can happen even if your daily activities won't make the cover of a "living large" magazine. When you awaken to the incredible miracles at play, you open your eyes to the deeper value of your purpose; you become motivated to serve the gift of fulfilling each day's potential.

This extraordinary journey is yours to embrace and cherish and savor and live. We could never really repay God for the gift of life, but every day we devote to living out our exceptional, irreplaceable, significant, personal paths, we get a bit closer to making good on the loan.

❖

Sometimes I try to repay you for this life with guilt-induced actions. I want to do my best from a place of gratitude. I want to serve my purpose for being with every day I am given. God, the idea that you have ordained this life for me, just me, as one of significance is all I need to inspire my next move…out of sincere gratitude.

Did That!

Checklists give us a sense of control and present finish lines for big and small accomplishments. I feel the power as I scratch off mundane things like washing my car, paying the mortgage, scheduling an appointment, etc. We tend to gravitate toward those solutions that seem simple: "Ten ways to improve your life," "Five steps to a new job."

God doesn't work this way. We're given some clear guidelines for living (like "Be kind to one another"), but it isn't for us to know how everything will unfold. Keep moving forward in faith and in God's will. Fulfillment will come. If you desperately need the thrill of a checklist, write on your heart every day to be faithful in your pursuit of God's purpose.

———◆———

I like to know what is coming, and I like to see clear steps toward the end result. It is probably from the days of college-course syllabi or multiple-choice tests. God, help me keep my focus on that one line, "Be faithful," and may I close each day with an offering of prayer and a very clear "Did that!"

Drop the Cash

If I made a movie loosely based on the end of life, it would have a scene with a bank robber getting caught midheist. He (or she) stands with a look of utter surprise as a magnified voice says, "Drop the money and come on out with your hands up."

While our end might not play out like this, I can guarantee that we will have to drop whatever material possessions are in our clutches. We will hopefully release our hold on things of this world eagerly. But are you willing to start letting go now? If you are clinging to material gain for your fulfillment, I have some advice: Drop the cash, and walk forward with your hands wide open to receive the life God has for you.

I confess, I do find my material blessings to be more than a comfort; they've become my security and my chance to say, "I have arrived." Give me a heart for a life richer than riches and more valuable than valuables. May I cling only to the wealth of spiritual treasures so that when my time does come...my hands are already lifted in praise to you.

Second Chances

I leave so many mistakes in my wake that I have grown to love mornings. I consider each one a second chance to do better and walk more closely in God's plan for me. Learning from our mistakes leads us to wiser choices later. But first we must pay attention to our mistakes. I know that it can seem best to bury them or leave them for others to stumble across. But if we claim them and consider them teachers, we can grow.

God is in the business of transformation. Acknowledge those mistakes and then release them to his custody this evening. And in the morning…use your second chance wisely.

———❖———

God, you must be tired of seeing these mistakes in my life. Forgive me for the sins that weigh me down. I give the errors, harsh words, white lies, bad decisions, and angry thoughts to you. I did them all. Please transform my mistakes today into stronger character and wisdom tomorrow.

A Life Half Fulfilled

I had a friend who went through a long portion of life without really seeing it. She was heartbroken, but the source of that pain was too difficult to look at closely. Even when we know things are not right, we are not necessarily able to discern what is wrong or what went wrong…all we know is the intimate relationship we develop with pain.

When you examine your life, what do you see? Is it empty? Is it whole and healed? Or have you looked lately? Spend time in prayer. Ask God to reveal what needs to be turned over to him to be repaired and restored.

I don't want to stop growing or feeling. God,
I need the security of your hope so that I can
safely examine my life. I don't want to be numb
as I carve out a path through the day. I want
passion and purpose. God, fill me up.

Empowerment

When we decide to live in the light of God, we receive our spiritual superpowers. Okay, that's probably not theologically sound…but our lives are improved, elevated beyond our prebelief existence. We have the power of the Holy Spirit at work in us and through us.

If you are living the same way with the same mind-set, choices, and power features, then you haven't yet started to live the transformed life. Are you afraid you won't recognize yourself if you give everything over to God? Is the "known" of the old, limited existence too comfortable to leave behind? The toughest life choice for some people is their initial acceptance of God—for others it is the decision to live a God-empowered life.

------◆------

Lord, I want to walk in your light. I see how my
way has not allowed for the changes that should
take place in my journey. Help me let go of the
fears so that I can experience transformation.

Going Home

Our geographic birthplace shapes who we are and notes where we've been. I spent my first eight years in a small Midwestern town that influenced my love for large climbing trees, broad front porches, and summer evenings at twilight.

Our spiritual birthplace shapes who we are and where we are going. You are born in God's heart and in his image and for his purpose. God's breath is your own. His miracles are found in the intricacies of your body and soul. The Creator knows that I love porches and trees and a night sky, just as he knows all about your deepest loves and longings. No matter how far this life journey takes you…you are always home and always heading home. This is the wonder of faith.

———◆———

You are my birthplace, my journey, my map, my compass, my past, my present, my future, my purpose, my heart, my salvation, my strength, my hope, my security, my joy, and my home. Thank you, Lord.

My Prayer Needs

ONE MINUTE WITH GOD

About the Author

Hope Lyda has worked in the publishing industry for ten years and is the author of several novels, including *Life, Libby, and the Pursuit of Happiness,* and numerous nonfiction titles such as the popular One-Minute Prayers series. When not writing her own books, Hope works as an editor helping others with their writing endeavors.

For more information about Hope and all of her books, stop by and visit her website: *www.hopelyda.com.*

Hope can be reached in care of

Harvest House Publishers
990 Owen Loop North
Eugene, OR 97402

Or by email at HopeLyda@yahoo.com